# 9 MUST-FOLLOW STEPS
## TO ESTABLISHING A THRIVING
## PRIVATE PRACTICE IN THE UK

HUYEN TRUONG, MBA

Paperback ISBN: 978-0-6458024-9-8
eBook ISBN: 978-0-6458024-8-1

# FOREWORD

Dear Cosmetic and Plastic Surgeons,

Let's be honest — building a successful cosmetic practice in the UK today takes more than medical expertise. It also requires a deep understanding of branding, marketing, business strategy, and the unique psychology of your patients. And yet, so many incredibly skilled doctors find themselves feeling stuck — not because they aren't brilliant at what they do, but because they're missing a clear path forward.

That's exactly why I wrote this eBook.

Think of it as a practical, step-by-step guide designed to help you grow your practice with clarity and confidence. No jargon. No vague advice. Just a solid roadmap to help you define your ideal patients, choose the right clinic location, build a standout brand, create a website that truly converts, and use smart digital marketing to bring the right people through your doors — and keep them coming back.

For more than a decade, I've had the privilege of working alongside some of the most respected cosmetic surgeons and aesthetic doctors around the world. I've seen firsthand what it takes to turn clinical excellence into a thriving, in-demand practice — and I want to share that with you.

Whether you're just starting out or ready to take your clinic to the next level, this guide is here to support you every step of the way.

I'm so glad you're here — let's get started.

Huyen Truong, MBA
Queen of Cosmetic Marketing
Division of Online Marketing For Doctors

# CONTENTS

# OPENING WORDS

Aesthetic clinics and cosmetic surgeries have grown into a multi-million-dollar entrepreneurial industry, not just in the UK, but globally. Demand for your services is higher than ever, which is excellent news for you as a cosmetic and plastic surgery clinic owner.

According to IBIS World, a foremost authority in business research, their October 2024 marketing data for Aesthetics Clinics in the UK indicates the cosmetic surgery industry is poised for exponential growth over the next five years.

This surge is attributed to the growing UK population, the ageing demographic, and the anticipated rise in obesity levels.

Additionally, social media has increased the social acceptance of these procedures, with more people seeking to look and feel their best.

There are now more people than ever wanting to have cosmetic procedures done, and **there is no sign of this slowing anytime soon.**

This guide is specifically tailored for plastic, reconstructive, and cosmetic surgeons who are either running their own private practices or considering a full transition to private practice in the future.

**It features interviews and quotes from successful practice owners within the UK market in the special bonus section at the end of this book.**

While there are many aspects to establishing a private practice—such as selecting locations, setting up facilities, acquiring technology, and managing insurance—this guide focuses primarily on the marketing and sales components. These elements are the lifeblood of your private practice, and we aim to share the insights we've gained through our experience working with practice owners.

For more detailed guidance on marketing for cosmetic and plastic surgeons, we recommend reading our globally published book, *Fully Booked* - Top Marketing Secrets Revealed To Dominate & Own Your Cosmetic Surgery Market

It is available on Kindle and Audible for your convenience.

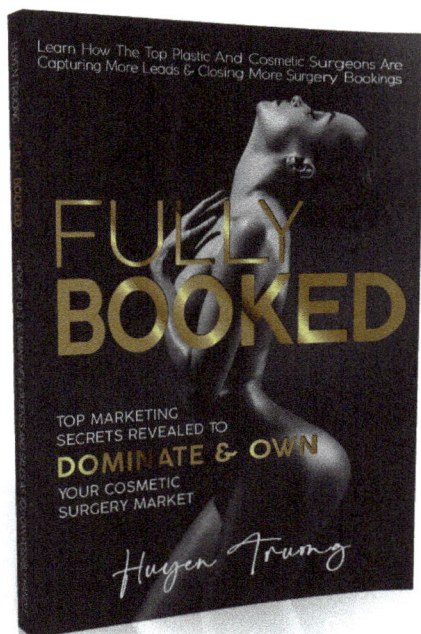

*Figure 1: Fully Booked - Our worldwide published book*

*Huyen Truong*

*Huyen Truong, MBA*
*Queen of Cosmetic Marketing*
*Online Marketing For Doctors*

# DETAILED MARKETING STRATEGIES
## FOR COSMETIC AND PLASTIC SURGEONS IN PRIVATE PRACTICE

To help build your confidence in transitioning to the private sector and accelerate the success of your private practice, we recommend taking the following steps. Achieving these milestones may take at least a year during the initial setup phase, so we suggest starting as soon as possible to see noticeable positive results—such as an increase in patient enquiries and bookings—by the second year.

Once you begin securing more bookings for the procedures you wish to perform and start seeing financial success, it will become easier to gather the resources needed to properly establish your private cosmetic surgery practice.

**The best time to start is now.**

## STEP 1. DEFINING YOUR TARGET MARKET: CORE SERVICES AND IDEAL PATIENTS

It's essential to be crystal clear about your practice's direction. Do you aim to be the leading provider of mummy makeover procedures in your area, or do you want to specialise in breast surgery or facelifts? Knowing precisely what type of practice you want to establish will help guide your marketing efforts and ensure you attract the right patients.

You also need to determine the types of patients you want to attract. Are you targeting privately insured patients or self-pay patients?

Consider the specific demographics, such as age groups, family situations, locations, hobbies, interests, and the communities they belong to. Being clear about your target audience early in the process will help you attract the right patients and shape your practice accordingly.

## STEP 2.  CHOOSING THE RIGHT LOCATION FOR YOUR CLINIC

At the start, you may not be in a position to purchase or rent an entire clinic space. Instead, consider renting a consulting room on an hourly basis at locations that are easily accessible to your prospective patients, close to your home, and within a network of good referral sources.

As we begin to build your clinic's online presence, particularly on Google, maintaining consistency across your chosen locations will help improve your rankings on Google Maps through local search engine optimisation.

Looking ahead, it's worth considering a location that can accommodate future growth, such as your own private operating theatre. I'll delve into this in more detail in the following section.

# STEP 3. DETERMINE PRICING FOR KEY PROCEDURES

## COST ANALYSIS AND CONTROL

When setting prices for cosmetic surgery procedures, it's important to consider three main components: 1) the surgeon and surgical assistant fees, 2) the hospital/theatre fee, and 3) the anaesthetist fee.

While you may have limited control over the anaesthetist's fee, you can adjust the surgeon's fee and the hospital or theatre costs. I don't recommend lowering your own fee, as your skills and experience should be appropriately rewarded. Lowering your prices signals that you lack other ways to stand out and are relying solely on cost to differentiate yourself from competitors.

However, you can look at ways to manage hospital and theatre expenses, which are often disproportionately high in the UK— sometimes even exceeding the surgeon's fee. While I understand the high operational costs these facilities face, cosmetic surgeries are typically not prioritised within these hospitals, adding further challenges.

In the long term, having your own theatre could be a game-changer, offering patients greater access to surgery slots and giving you a clear advantage in terms of cost management.

Although setting up a private theatre may seem expensive initially, you could share the facility with other clinics or surgeons to distribute the costs, or even sublet it to other practices to generate additional income.

To maintain neutrality and avoid concerns from other surgeons about patient competition, the theatre could operate under a separate name and website, independent of your clinic's branding.

This way, it can be marketed as a standalone entity, appealing to both the cosmetic and plastic surgery community as well as other medical professionals seeking an affordable solution for surgical and non-surgical procedures.

As an example, Mr Ahmed Ali-Khan, the owner of LASE Cosmetic in Jesmond, Newcastle, UK, recently shared at the BAAPS event that his private general anaesthetic (GA) theatre became profitable within a year of obtaining its licence, with 90% of the clinic's procedures being GA cases.

This demonstrates that owning your own GA theatre could significantly enhance the success of your private practice.

Example of private operating theatre for rental web page:

https://www.canovamedical.com/about/operating-theatre-rental/
https://deltaclinics.co.uk/theatre-rentals/
https://www.thelakeclinic.co.uk/treatments/theatre-rental/

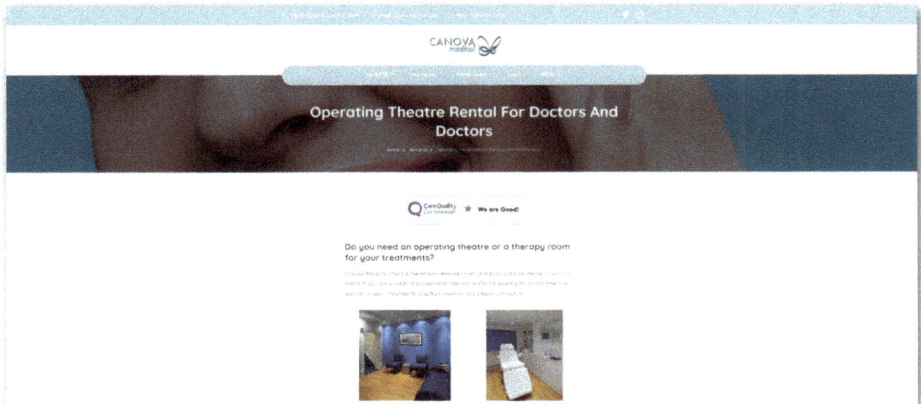

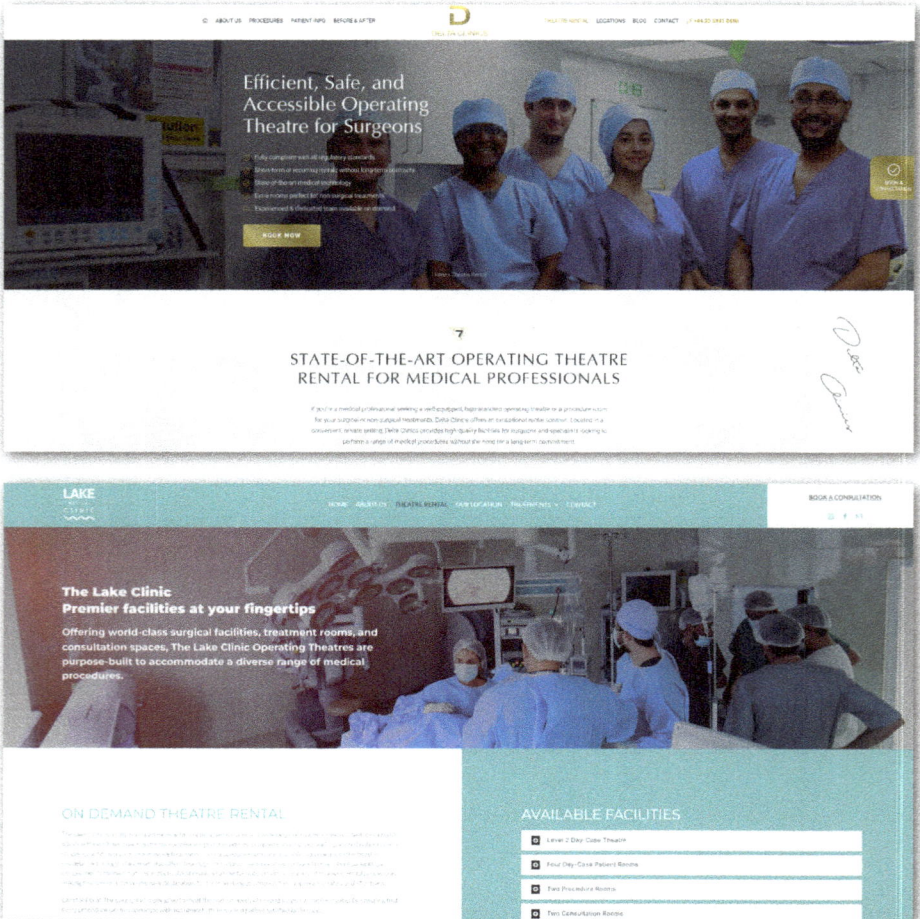

Figure 2: 3 Web pages of UK private operating theatre for rental

## PAYMENT PLAN SOLUTIONS FOR HIGH-VALUE PROCEDURES

Cosmetic surgeries often come with significant costs, and while many patients are eager to proceed with their desired procedures, they may not have immediate access to the necessary funds.

Offering payment plans can help you convert more consultations into confirmed procedure bookings. Below are a few options you can provide to prospective patients:

## PAYMENT ARRANGEMENT BEFORE YOUR SURGERY

Before the patient's surgery, they can consider implementing a Payment Plan or a Surgery Savings Plan. A special-purpose savings fund allows them to save up the required funds before the operation.

## PRE-PAY FOR SURGERY

Pre-paying for your services in advance through instalments can offer several advantages for patients seeking cosmetic surgery. By choosing this option, patients have the opportunity to plan and budget for their surgery. This can make the process more financially manageable. Instead of having to pay the full amount upfront, spreading the cost over instalments can alleviate financial strain.

This prepayment option allows patients to secure their surgery date and avoid potential price increases in the future. It provides peace of mind, knowing that the surgery is already taken care of. Patients can focus on their recovery without worrying about financial aspects post-surgery.

Moreover, pre-paying in instalments can offer flexibility to patients, allowing them to choose a payment schedule that aligns with their financial situation. Whether it's a weekly, monthly, or customised payment plan, this approach offers convenience and adaptability.

Before opting for this payment method, it is essential for your clinic to discuss the terms and conditions of the instalment plan with patients. Being fully informed about the payment schedule, interest rates (if applicable), and any associated fees can help patients make an informed decision.

Patients should also enquire about any refund or cancellation policies related to prepayment. This ensures they are aware of the options available in case of unforeseen circumstances.

Overall, pre-paying for your services in advance through instalments can offer financial convenience. It is an option worth considering for those who seek a well-planned and financially manageable cosmetic surgery journey.

## PAYMENT PLANS, MEDICAL CREDIT AND FINANCE OPTIONS

We acknowledge that not everyone may have the funds readily available to pay for their surgery upfront. Independent finance companies can offer various medical credit and financing options.

These medical credit and finance options can provide a practical solution for patients seeking plastic surgery but prefer a more flexible payment approach. By working with reputable finance companies, patients have the opportunity to explore tailored payment plans that suit their individual financial circumstances.

Applying for medical credit or finance allows patients to break down the total cost of their surgery into more manageable monthly instalments. This alleviates the need to pay the entire amount at once, making the financial burden more manageable.

Before opting for medical credit or financing, it's crucial for patients to carefully review the terms and conditions. This includes understanding interest rates, any applicable fees, and the overall cost of borrowing. Being well-informed ensures that patients are comfortable with the financial arrangements and can make informed decisions about their surgery journey.

If you need help in terms of finding the current best financial plan companies in the UK, please reach out to our team at marketing@ onlinemarketingfordoctors.com.

## STEP 4. CREATE A PROFESSIONAL STRONG BRANDING FOR YOUR CLINIC

Your brand is arguably one of your organisation's most important assets. It gives your organisation an identity, makes your clinic memorable, encourages prospects to buy from you, supports your marketing and advertising, and brings your employees pride.

One of the most common mistakes when setting up a new clinic, branding wasn't done properly, giving the clinic an unclear identity about who you are, how you want to be perceived in the prospects' eyes and how you are different from other clinics.

- Create a unique selling proposition (USP) that sets you apart from other surgeons or plastic surgery clinics.

- Define your specialty areas within cosmetic surgery.

- Develop a consistent brand voice and visual identity across all platforms.

- Consider working with a branding expert or marketing agency specialising in medical aesthetics.

## BRANDING VS. MARKETING

While it's easy to combine branding and marketing into one discipline, they're quite distinct. Put simply, branding is the identity of a clinic, and marketing includes the tactics and strategies, which communicate that vision.

Branding shapes how prospective patients perceive a service or product.

A strong brand image can create positive associations with quality, value, or a particular lifestyle, influencing purchasing decisions.

In fact, 71% of consumers (particularly Gen Z) say they're more likely to buy from brands they trust. Meanwhile, prior surveys we ran also showed that their purchases could also be influenced by brands with shared values.

## HOW BRAND TRUST AFFECTS SHOPPING: A LONDON STORY

One day, while walking in London, I saw an Amazon Fresh store. I've been using Amazon online for over 10 years, so I was curious about their grocery shop.

I thought about why I like Amazon: lots of choices, easy checkout, reliability, and new ideas. These things made me trust the company over the years.

I decided to buy a few things from the store. It was different from normal UK supermarkets, both in what they sold and how you shop.

This made me realise something important: we're more likely to buy from brands we trust. I went into the Amazon Fresh store because I trusted Amazon from my online shopping experiences.

For doctors, especially cosmetic surgeons, there's a lesson here. If you create a strong identity for your clinic based on values that matter to your patients, your marketing will work more effectively.

A clear brand identity helps guide your marketing. It lets you connect better with potential patients. When done well, this approach not only brings in new clients but turns them into brand advocates who recommend you to others.

In short, my trust in Amazon's grocery store is like the trust patients might have in a well-known cosmetic surgery clinic. Building and keeping this trust is a powerful way to market your services, beyond just using ads.

*Figure 3: I came back from Amazon Fresh in London with a bag of goodies*

# DEVELOPING A STRONG BRAND FOR COSMETIC CLINIC

## 1. Create a Unique Selling Proposition (USP)

Your USP is what sets you apart from other surgeons or clinics. To develop a compelling USP:

- Identify your strengths and unique skills. Do you have a particular technique or approach that yields exceptional results?

- Consider your patient demographics. Do you specialise in serving a specific group?

- Reflect on your values and philosophy. What drives your practice beyond just medical expertise?

- Think about patient pain points. How do you address these better than others?

Examples of USPs:

- "Combining artistry with surgical precision for natural-looking results"

- "Specialising in minimally invasive techniques for faster recovery"

- "Personalised care from consultation to post-operative follow-up"

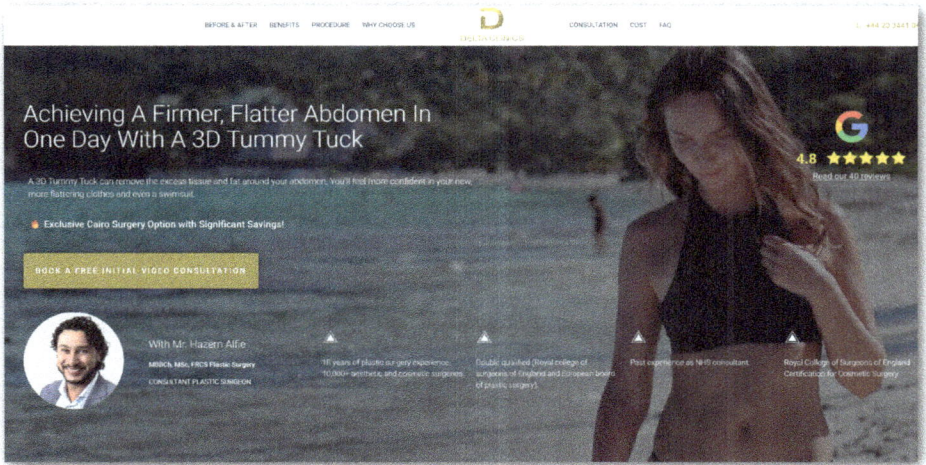

Figure 4: Example of Delta Clinics UK with their strong USP for their 3D Contour Tummy Tuck

https://lp.deltaclinics.co.uk/tummy-tuck/

## 2. Define Your Specialty Areas

While you may be qualified in various procedures, focusing on specific areas can strengthen your brand:

- Choose procedures you excel at or have extensive experience in.

- Consider emerging trends or procedures with growing demand.

- Look for gaps in the market in your geographical area.

- Align your specialties with your passion and expertise.

For example:

- "London's leading expert in ethnic rhinoplasty"

- "Pioneering non-surgical facial rejuvenation techniques"

- "Specialising in body contouring after major weight loss"

## 3. Develop a Consistent Brand Voice and Visual Identity

Consistency across all platforms helps build recognition and trust:

- Brand Voice:

  - Decide on the tone: Professional? Warm and approachable? Innovative and cutting-edge?

  - Use consistent language in all communications, from your website to social media posts.

  - Develop a set of key messages that reflect your USP and values.

- Visual Identity:

  - Create a professional logo that represents your brand.

  - Choose a colour palette and stick to it across all materials.

  - Use consistent fonts and design elements.

  - Ensure all imagery (photos, videos) reflects your brand aesthetic.

  - Maintain a cohesive look across your website, social media, brochures, and office decor.

## 4. Work with Branding Experts

Collaborating with professionals can elevate your branding efforts:

- Branding Expert:

  - Can help distil your unique attributes into a cohesive brand strategy.

  - Assists in developing your USP and key messaging.

- Ensure your brand resonates with your target audience.

- Marketing Agency Specialising in Medical Aesthetics:

  - Understands the unique challenges and opportunities in cosmetic surgery marketing.

  - Can develop targeted campaigns that comply with medical advertising regulations.

  - Provides expertise in digital marketing strategies specific to the aesthetics industry.

  - Offers insights into current trends and patient behaviours in the cosmetic surgery market.

When choosing to work with experts:

- Look for professionals with experience in the medical or cosmetic surgery field.

- Ask for case studies or examples of their work with other surgeons or clinics.

- Ensure they understand the ethical considerations and regulations in medical marketing.

- Discuss how they can help you stand out in a competitive market while maintaining professionalism.

Remember, your brand should authentically represent you and your practice. It should resonate with your ideal patients and differentiate you in the competitive field of cosmetic surgery.

## STEP 5. BUILD A WEBSITE THAT CONVERTS & REFLECTS YOUR EXPERTISE

One of the most common mistakes I've seen is clinics having outdated websites. They spend a lot of money on marketing to drive traffic to these sites and then wonder why they aren't getting many bookings.

When it comes to promoting a medical clinic online, your website serves as the foundation for all digital marketing activities and acts as your primary online storefront. However, many practices overlook the importance of having a functional website capable of consistently generating new patients.

*First of all, I'd like to ask you what is your biggest frustration with your website? Do you?*

- Not have enough leads

- Have Low quality or unqualified leads

- Turning leads into patients

- Competition is killing us

- All of the answers above

If you selected all of the answers above, it indicates that your website is experiencing both traffic and conversion issues, which is quite common based on our observation of thousands of medical websites over the years.

If your website traffic is below 500 visits per month, it suggests a traffic problem. When your website lacks sufficient visitors, the likelihood of attracting an adequate number of prospective patients decreases. Coupled with the low conversion rate of your website, this explains why you're experiencing a low and inconsistent flow of new patients.

### *Secondly, does the quality of your website reflect the quality of your work?*

- Yes, my website looks incredible

- No, my website looks like it's from 1999

After over a decade of working with medical clinics, I've realised that one of the main reasons patients don't book is because the perceived value of the procedure isn't greater than the price.

Meaning the website is not building up the perceived value of your services so when users see your website looking dated and aesthetically unpleasing, it would align with how prospective patients perceive your clinic.

Showcase a tour of your gorgeous office and surgical suite, your rapid recovery process, and your superior aftercare support on your website via video presentation that would be more impressive.

This should be done even before prospects begin enquiring about the first consultation. The value needs to be established through all touchpoints, from the premium appearance of the website to the use of authentic, high-quality videos and images across both the website and social media platforms.

Since we are offering high-value procedures, consider the experience when walking into luxury stores like Hermes, Louis Vuitton, or Burberry. What is your initial impression? It's the ambiance of space and luxury, isn't it? And what do you expect to pay? You would expect to pay more right? Similarly, your website must exude a premium look to enhance the perceived value of your clinic and procedures.

These are the essential elements your website should include:

## 1. Ensure your website is mobile-responsive and user-friendly

In today's digital age, it's crucial that your website performs well on all devices, particularly mobile phones.

- Implement a responsive design that adapts to various screen sizes.

- Ensure fast loading times. Slow websites can frustrate potential patients and harm your search engine rankings.

- Use a clean, intuitive layout. Avoid cluttered designs that might overwhelm visitors.

- Whenever possible, avoid using stock images. Instead, opt for original photos and videos to strengthen your website's credibility and enhance your brand's unique identity.

- Make navigation straightforward. Users should be able to find key information within a few clicks.

- Include clear calls-to-action (CTAs) throughout the site, such as "Book a Consultation" or "Learn More About This Procedure".

- Ensure accessibility for users with disabilities, adhering to Web Content Accessibility Guidelines (WCAG).

## 2. Include detailed information about procedures, your qualifications, and patient testimonials

Transparency builds trust with potential patients.

- Provide comprehensive information about each procedure you offer. Explain the process, expected outcomes, recovery time, and potential risks.

- Highlight your qualifications, including education, training, certifications, and memberships in professional bodies like the British Association of Aesthetic Plastic Surgeons (BAAPS).

- Include a detailed CV or professional biography.

- Feature patient testimonials prominently. Ensure these comply with General Medical Council (GMC) guidelines on using patient feedback in marketing.

- Consider including video testimonials for a more personal touch, but always obtain proper consent.

## 3. Showcase high-quality before-and-after galleries

Visual evidence of your work can be highly persuasive.

- Organise galleries by procedure type for easy navigation.

- Use high-quality, professional photographs. Consistency in lighting and positioning is key.

- Ensure all images are authentic and unedited. Misleading imagery can damage trust and may violate advertising standards.

- Include brief descriptions with each set of images, noting the specific procedure performed.

- Obtain written consent from patients before using their images, in line with UK data protection laws.

## 4. Implement SEO best practices to improve visibility in search results

Optimising your site for search engines can significantly increase your online visibility.

- Conduct keyword research to identify terms potential patients are using to search for cosmetic surgery services in your area.

- Optimise your content for these keywords, but ensure it reads naturally.

- Create unique, informative meta titles and descriptions for each page.

- Use header tags (H1, H2, etc.) to structure your content logically.

- Ensure your site has a logical internal linking structure.

- Optimise images with descriptive file names and alt text.

- Create location-specific pages if you operate in multiple areas.

- Regularly update your content to keep it fresh and relevant.

## 5. Include a blog with regular updates on cosmetic surgery topics

A blog can establish you as an authority in your field and improve your site's SEO (Search Engine Optimisation).

- Write about trending topics in cosmetic surgery, new techniques, or common patient concerns.

- Aim for a mix of content: educational articles, procedure spotlights, patient stories (with consent), and industry news.

- Update regularly - aim for at least one new post per week.

- Use your blog to answer frequently asked questions from patients.

- Encourage engagement by allowing comments, but moderate them carefully.

- Share your blog posts on your social media channels to increase reach.

## 6. Offer easy online booking for consultations

Make it as simple as possible for potential patients to take the next step.

- Implement a user-friendly online booking system.

- Ensure the booking process is secure and GDPR-compliant.

- Offer multiple appointment options to cater to different schedules.

- Send automatic confirmation emails with all necessary information.

- Include a contact number for those who prefer to book by phone.

- Consider offering virtual consultation options for initial screenings.

- Implement a reminder system to reduce no-shows.

Remember, your website is often a potential patient's first impression of your practice. It should reflect the high standards and professionalism of your in-person services. Regularly review and update your site to ensure it remains current and effective.

## STEP 6.  BUILD YOUR ONLINE REPUTATION WITH INDEPENDENT REVIEWS

Our next secret for building a successful private practice in your chosen niche is to get this audience of current and previous patients working for you. You need to get them to build your online reputation by writing positive reviews about you, your services and your practice.

Any positive review is extremely beneficial to your reputation. But if you want to dominate your niche, you need to generate more positive reviews than your competitors are.

Let me ask you a few simple questions;

- Do you know what your patients are saying about you online?

- Do you have a strong five-star reputation?

- Are you personally responding to negative reviews?

- Do you have a strategy to gain more five-star reviews?

Prospective patients can be incredibly thorough when researching for a surgeon. After all, surgery is a big undertaking! One of the very first things many of them will do is Google "your name + reviews".

If you haven't done this already yourself... you should. Now is the time to see what people have been saying about you online. What you find, can make or break your ability to gain new patients.

All of those advertising dollars could be going to waste if someone wants to find reviews of your services online, and they come across something like this...

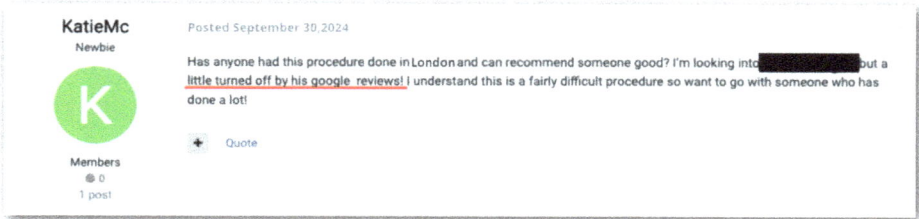

*Figure 5: Online Review - September 2024*

If your prospective patients can't find you, or even worse, if all they see are negative reviews or just a few non-descript reviews when they are searching you out online, they will most likely just move on to the next surgeon that they are thinking of going to see for a consultation.

So, the question is... how do you build your online reputation?

First, we need a spot where we want to direct your patients to leave their reviews. My recommendation is to turn to these 3rd party review platform websites for the medical profession;

1. www.google.com/mybusiness

2. www.realself.com

3. www.topdoctors.co.uk/doctor/plastic-surgery

4. www.doctify.com/uk

I recommend these websites because typically they will appear first when someone searches for your name looking for reviews. But you can also consider other local directories in your area that allow post-op patients the opportunity to review your services honestly in a search engine-approved testimonial format.

There are also many other online forums, chat groups, and social media networks for patients to share their stories and recommend surgeons to other members. These areas also have a frequency towards criticising surgeons, which is why you should have someone on your team monitoring these areas for bad reviews.

The reason testimonials on 3rd party sites are credible and can help influence your standing, is that they are independent. People can be upfront and honest about their experiences. Genuine online testimonials are the digital equivalent of a positive word-of-mouth referral.

Which is better than an anonymous testimonial on your practice's website that someone could think was fabricated or that could have been posted by anyone.

Remember your potential patients aren't necessarily going to look at the most immediate spots for help or answers, they are savvier than that. They will be looking for clear independent non-influenced feedback for establishing concrete proof that they can trust you.

## Engage with Prospective Patients by Answering Questions on Third-Party Review Platforms

Participating in third-party reviewing platforms like RealSelf can significantly enhance a plastic surgeon's online presence and patient acquisition. These platforms serve as valuable resources for prospective patients seeking unbiased information about cosmetic procedures.

By actively engaging on these forums, surgeons can demonstrate their expertise by answering questions and providing insights on various treatments. This not only establishes credibility but also allows potential patients to get a sense of the surgeon's approach and communication style.

These platforms typically feature extensive galleries of before-and-after photos, which are crucial in the decision-making process for many patients considering cosmetic surgery.

By contributing to these galleries, surgeons can showcase their work to a wide audience of interested individuals. The ability for patients to compare qualified surgeons and read honest reviews about whether specific treatments are "Worth It" creates a transparent environment that can build trust and confidence in a surgeon's abilities.

Moreover, participation in these forums keeps surgeons abreast of the latest aesthetic treatment news and trends, ensuring they remain at the forefront of their field. This engagement can lead to increased visibility, more patient enquiries, and ultimately, a growing practice.

The combination of influencer marketing and active participation in reputable third-party reviewing platforms creates a comprehensive digital strategy that can significantly boost a plastic surgeon's online presence and patient acquisition efforts.

I'll elaborate on influencer marketing later in this book.

## How Do I Get More Online Patient Reviews?

I could write a whole book just on reputation management. It is a very broad, and quickly evolving space. But fundamentally the challenge is the same for everyone; *"How do I get more online testimonials?"*.

Simply put, you will get more by encouraging and empowering your patients to write reviews about their experiences with you on independent forums, like the ones I listed earlier. Let's break down the best means available to you;

1. **Ask them in person**

    If a patient seems happy with their results following your services, you need to feel comfortable with asking that patient for a review. It may feel taboo, but most people are accustomed to being asked; everyone is asking for a review these days, from Uber to their supermarket.

    Emphasise that this will mean a lot for you personally, and you'd be appreciative of them writing a review for you. Too many surgeons won't ask, and you need to move past that if that includes you, especially if you really want to lift your credibility and your practice.

## 2. Have it done at your office

While the patient is waiting for you in the waiting room for a follow-up meeting, that is a great time to ask them to write you an independent review. This could be done through the help of the practice manager, or even by leaving an iPad or computer setup in the space. Make it as easy as possible for your patient.

## 3. Postcards

If you aren't comfortable with having to directly ask for a review in options 1 or 2, hand out thank you cards requesting a review and listing the sites where they can be left on.

## 4. Emails

And finally, as part of any post-operative care emails that you send, make sure you directly ask for a review. Please also keep in mind to follow up as well.

As I said before, the fortune is made in the follow-up. And patients who have stuck with you, and kept supporting you beyond their immediate needs, are much more likely to leave a review—and a positive one at that.

Getting reviews isn't easy; *you'll need to work just as hard for reviews as you do to deliver your services.* Make the process clear and easy for your patients, and don't be shy with asking. Your online reputation is too critical to your success to leave to chance, and changes won't happen overnight.

But by getting started today, establishing a process and laying the foundation for a consistent process of encouraging more reviews, you'll start seeing exponential growth in your patient numbers as your reviews continue to promote you and your services on your behalf.

## STEP 7.  LEVERAGE SOCIAL MEDIA FOR VISIBILITY & TRUST

Are you a plastic surgeon looking to make your mark on social media? With the aesthetic industry growing, it's more important than ever to set your plastic surgery clinic apart from the crowd. Today, we're diving into how you can shine on platforms like Instagram, Facebook, YouTube and TikTok.

Let's kick things off with something that's often overlooked but incredibly crucial: your social media profile.

### First Impressions Count: Having a Clear Bio on Your Profile

Think of your bio as your digital handshake. It's the first thing potential patients see when they land on your profile, so you want to make it count!

Start by highlighting your specialisations. What specific plastic surgery procedures do you offer? This immediately sets you apart from general aesthetics clinics. Maybe you're known for your rhinoplasties or perhaps you're a breast augmentation expert. Whatever it is, make sure it's front and centre.

Next, don't be shy about your credentials. You've worked hard for those qualifications, so show them off! Mention your board certifications and years of experience. This builds trust right from the get-go.

Remember, your bio should speak directly to your target audience. Are you specialising in mummy makeovers? Make sure that comes across. Tailoring your bio to your ideal patient demographic helps the right people find you.

Finally, include a clear call to action. Encourage profile visitors to book a consultation or learn more about your procedures. Make it easy for them to take the next step.

Another top tip is to make sure you're using all the features within a platform. On Instagram for example, you can add Highlight galleries. Consider creating a highlight about you & your qualifications and experience, or another showcasing your past work in any specific procedure. This will help you immediately communicate the specific type of clinic you are and the procedures you offer.

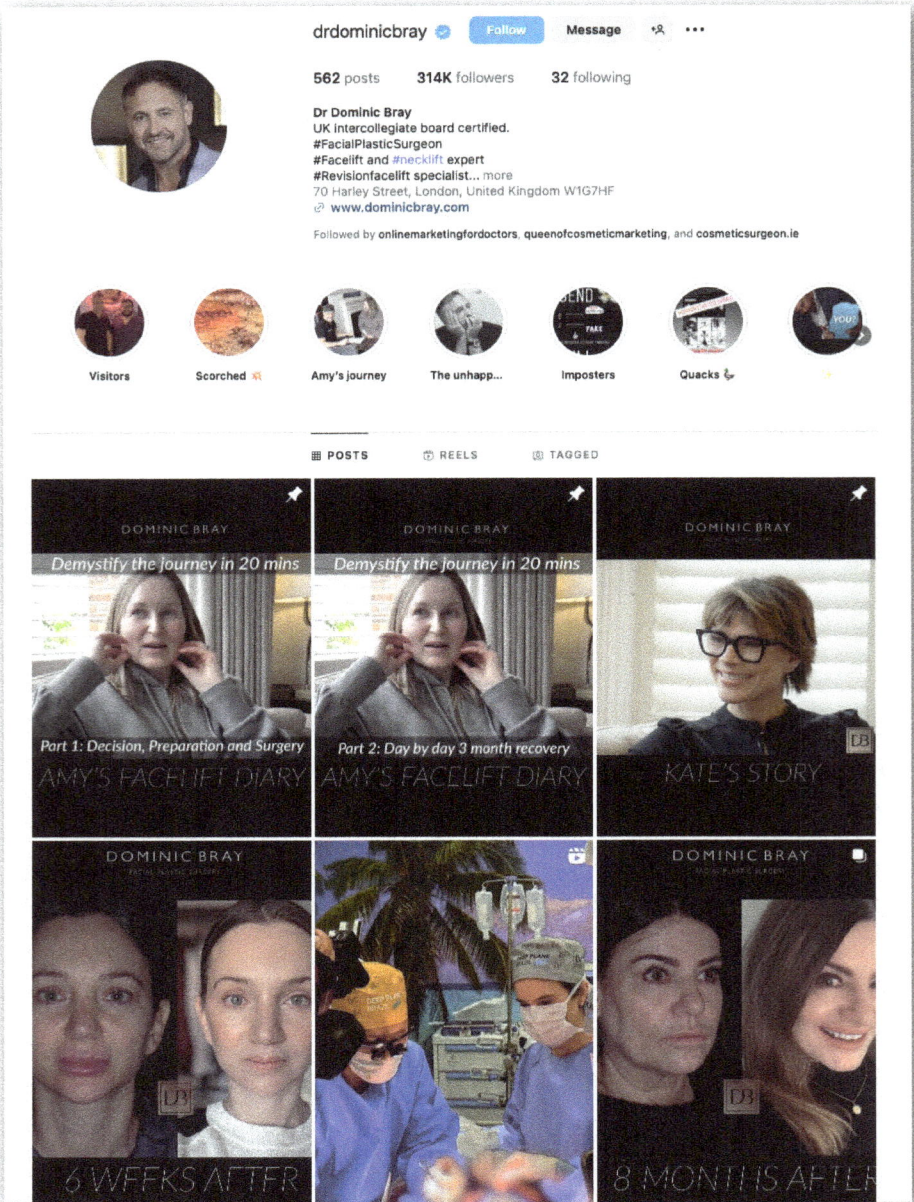

Figure 6: Screenshot of Dr Dominic Bray's Instagram Page - Facelift Expert

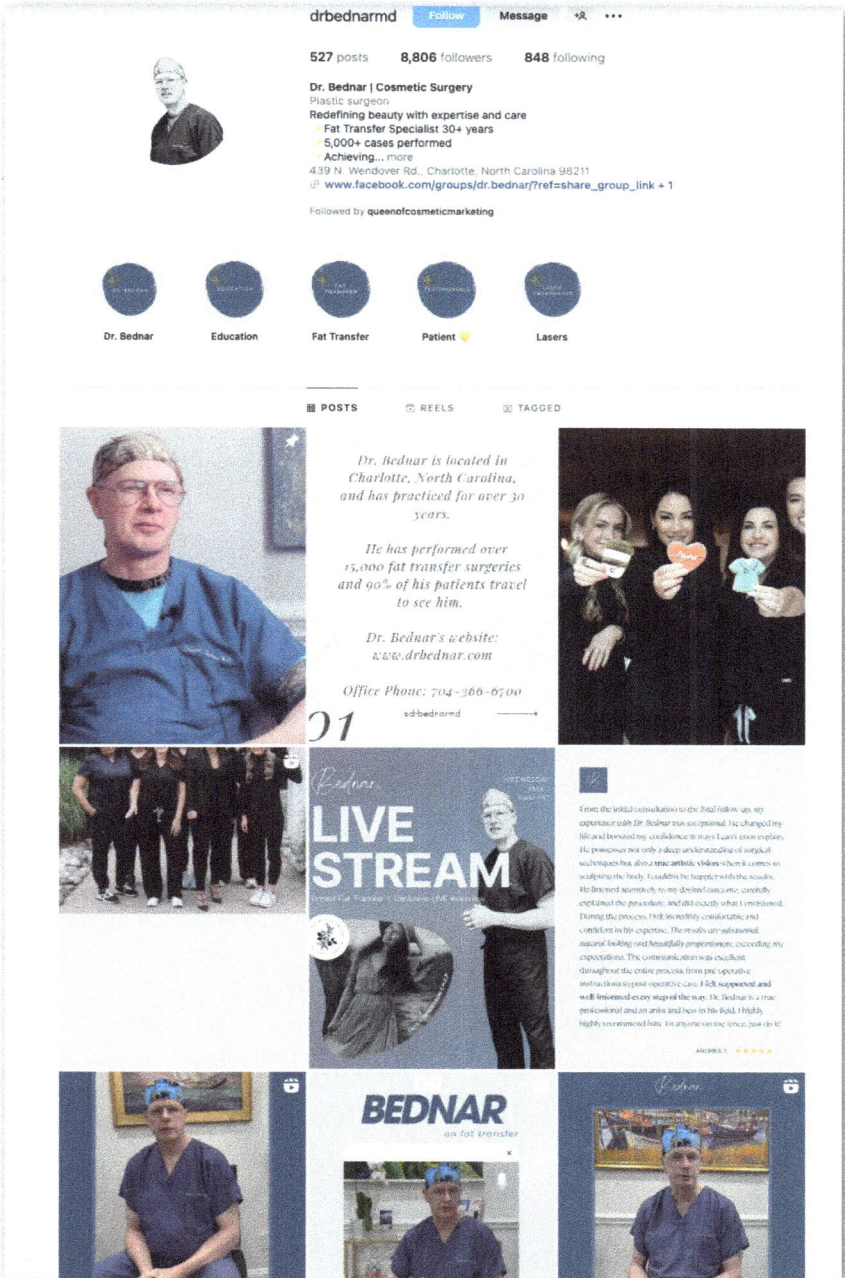

*Figure 7: Screenshot of Dr Bednar's Instagram Page - Fat Transfer to Breast Expert*

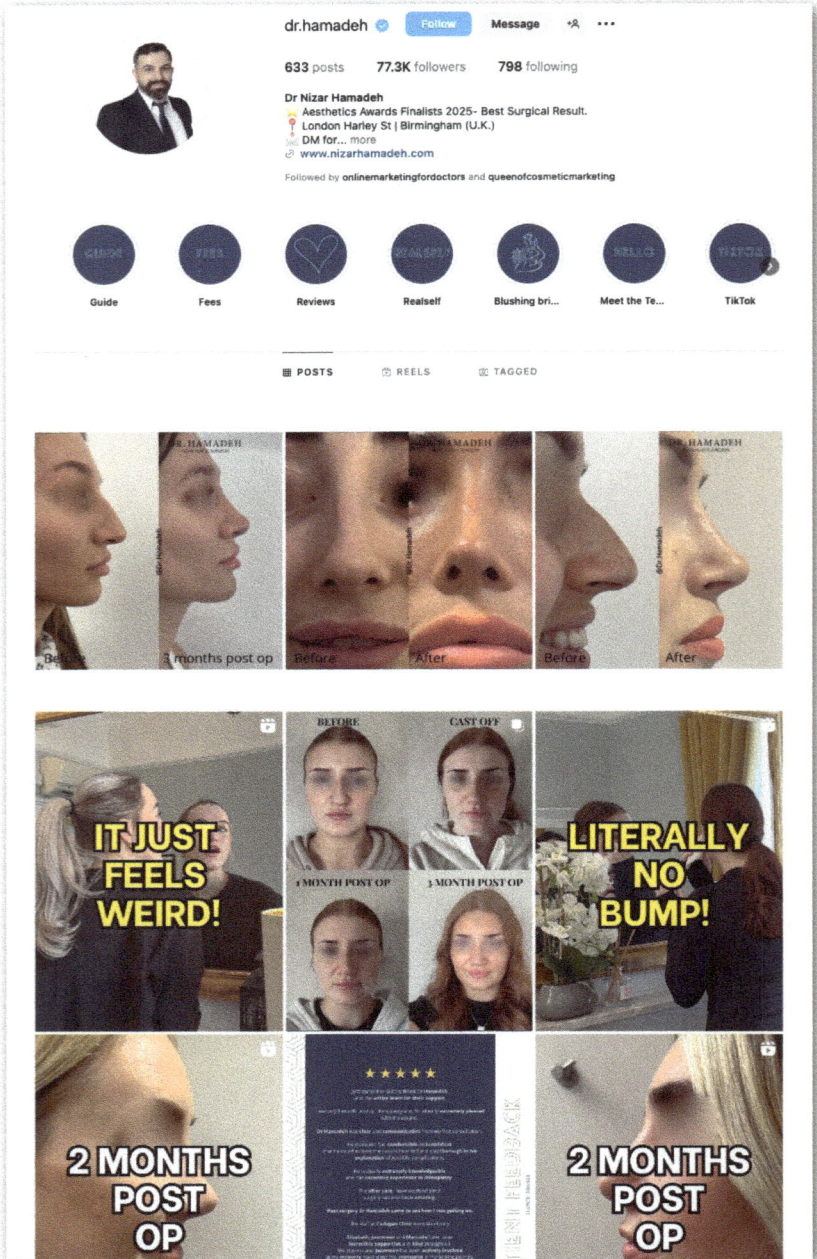

*Figure 8: Screenshot of Dr Hamadeh's Instagram Page - Rhinoplasty Expert*

## Positioning and Messaging: Making it Clear Who You Are, What You Offer

Now, let's talk about how you position yourself in the vast sea of aesthetic practitioners.

First and foremost, establish your authority. Position your clinic as a leader in plastic surgery, not just aesthetics. Share your unique approach or philosophy that sets you apart. Maybe you have a particular technique that yields amazing results, or perhaps you're known for your natural-looking outcomes. Whatever it is, make sure it comes across in your messaging.

Education is also key. Use your platform to share informative posts about plastic surgery procedures, risks, recovery, and patient journeys. This not only showcases your expertise but also helps potential patients make informed decisions. Remember, an educated patient is often a confident and satisfied patient.

Social media platforms have advanced algorithms to help connect your content to the right audience. For example, when you upload an Instagram Reel with captions, the algorithm can use the keywords in your captions to connect to people interested in your specific niche.

## Content Strategy: Post Consistently Around Some Core Topics

Now, let's dive into the meat of your social media presence - your content. What you post is the easiest way for visitors to your profile to quickly understand and differentiate your work and expertise. Consistency is key, but what you post matters just as much as how often you post.

Let's start with procedure-focused content. This is your bread and butter. Create in-depth posts about specific procedures you offer. Include before-and-after photos - these are gold in the plastic surgery world. Add patient testimonials and address FAQs. This gives potential patients a comprehensive look at what you offer and what they can expect. Short form video is a great medium for this too. Check out our recent video on this topic.

Don't be afraid to put yourself in the spotlight too. Share your background, your philosophy, your approach to plastic surgery. This humanises your brand and builds a personal connection with your audience. People want to know the person behind the scalpel!

Patient stories are another powerful tool. Share authentic experiences and transformations, but don't just focus on the physical changes. Highlight the emotional benefits of plastic surgery. How did it boost their confidence? How did it change their life? This helps potential patients envision their own transformations.

Now, let's talk about video content. Platforms like TikTok and Instagram Reels are perfect for engaging, educational content. Use these to showcase quick tips, debunk myths, or give sneak peeks into your procedures. Short-form video is huge right now, so don't miss out on this opportunity.

And don't forget about behind-the-scenes content. Give your audience glimpses into your clinic's culture, introduce them to your team, and show off your state-of-the-art facilities. This builds trust and transparency, making potential patients feel more comfortable with your practice.

Remember, the key to standing out on social media is to be authentic, consistent, and valuable to your audience. Don't just sell procedures – build relationships, educate, and inspire.

## 1. Focus on visually-oriented platforms like Instagram, Facebook, TikTok, and YouTube

Each platform offers unique opportunities for engaging potential patients:

- **Instagram:** Ideal for sharing high-quality images and short videos. Use a mix of posts, Stories, and Reels to showcase your work and personality.

  - Curate a visually appealing feed that reflects your brand aesthetic.

  - Use relevant hashtags to increase discoverability, e.g., #CosmeticSurgeryUK, #LondonPlasticSurgeon #deepplanefacelift #fattransfertobreast...etc

- **Facebook:** Excellent for community building and sharing longer-form content.

  - Create a business page to share updates, articles, and events.

  - Utilise Facebook Groups to engage with patients and answer questions.

- **TikTok:** Growing in popularity, especially among younger audiences.

  - Create short, engaging videos explaining procedures or debunking myths.

- Participate in trending challenges when appropriate to increase visibility.

- **YouTube:** Perfect for in-depth video content.

  - Share procedure explanations, patient testimonials, and educational content.

  - Consider starting a regular Q&A series to address common patient concerns.

Remember to tailor your content to each platform's unique audience and style.

## 2. Share before-and-after photos and video content of procedures

Visual content is crucial in cosmetic surgery marketing, but must be handled ethically:

- Always obtain explicit, written consent from patients before sharing their images or videos.

- Ensure all shared content complies with General Medical Council (GMC) guidelines on using social media.

- Use consistent lighting and positioning in before-and-after photos for accurate representation.

- Consider using 3D imaging or animation to demonstrate procedures when actual patient images aren't available.

- Include detailed captions explaining the procedure, recovery time, and realistic expectations.

- Share 'journey' content, showing progress at different stages post-procedure.

- Be mindful of platform-specific regulations regarding medical content. Some platforms may have stricter rules about showing surgical procedures.

### 3. Use Instagram Stories and Reels for behind-the-scenes content and quick tips

These features offer a more casual, immediate way to connect with your audience:

- Share 'day in the life' content to humanise your practice.

- Use the 'Question' sticker in Stories to host regular Q&A sessions.

- Create educational Reels explaining common procedures or addressing myths.

- Share patient testimonials (with consent) as short video clips.

- Highlight your team members and their expertise.

- Use Stories to promote new blog posts or upcoming events.

- Save key Stories as Highlights for easy access on your profile.

### 4. Engage with followers by responding to comments and messages promptly

Building a community is crucial for social media success:

- Aim to respond to all comments and direct messages within 24 hours.

- Use a warm, professional tone in all interactions.

- Address negative comments or reviews professionally and offer to take the conversation private when necessary.

- Create a FAQ document to ensure consistent responses to common queries.

- Use social listening tools to monitor mentions of your practice across platforms.

- Encourage your team to engage as well, fostering a sense of community around your practice.

- Remember that all online interactions should comply with patient confidentiality standards.

## 5. Consider paid social media advertising to reach potential patients

Paid advertising can significantly expand your reach:

- Use platform-specific ad tools to target your ideal patient demographic.

- Create separate ad campaigns for different procedures or services.

- Use compelling visuals and clear calls-to-action in your ads.

- Experiment with different ad formats (e.g., carousel ads, video ads) to see what resonates with your audience.

- Implement retargeting campaigns to re-engage users who have visited your website.

- Ensure all ad content complies with both platform guidelines and UK advertising standards for medical procedures.

- Monitor ad performance regularly and adjust your strategy based on results.

- Consider hiring a specialist in medical advertising to optimise your campaigns.

Remember, while social media can be a powerful marketing tool, it's crucial to maintain professional standards and ethical practices at all times. All content should be factual, responsible, and in line with GMC guidelines on social media use for medical professionals.

## STEP 8. USE EVERGREEN CONTENT TO DOMINATE SEARCH & SOCIAL PLATFORMS

*"Good marketing makes the company look smart, great marketing makes the customer feel smart"*
—Joe Chernow

### Content Is King

If you want to be at the top of your niche, you have to establish yourself as the go-to person for that category in terms of content.

Why?

Because content is king.

Through content, you can make your prospective patients feel smart by educating them and giving them all of the content that they could possibly need or find about your niche.

You might be thinking, *"Whoa… Huyen, I've already published a website, isn't it enough?"*.

The website was just a great foundational starting point to build your successful private practice. You need to continuously produce new and valued content to keep up your expert status and to continuously stay ahead of your competition.

Nobody got labelled as the GOAT (Greatest Of All Time) in their respective industry by just stopping after their first taste of success. Instead…they continuously worked hard on their game, or making new hits or in a surgeon's case – staying informed and educated on the trends, challenges and opportunities in your industry.

Your job as the celebrity authority is to do the same. In order to maintain and grow your celebrity authority status, you have to keep pushing forward.

In this 4th move, I'm going to outline exactly what you need to do to produce more "hits" and how to get thousands of people following you and your content online, so you can completely dominate all social and search channels, leaving your competition in the dust.

## Value-Based Marketing – The Marketing Choice For Plastic and Cosmetic Surgeons

One early morning years ago, as part of my morning ritual, I started reading some marketing articles online and came across a webinar talking about value-based marketing, and how it started in 1948.

Value-based marketing is based on the simple premise of "giving before asking". People are 10 times more likely to come to you to learn something, than they are to be sold something. It is an appeal to a prospective patient's values and ethics. It shifts marketing from a practice-centric approach to a patient-centric one.

Marketing is often seen as "showing off". Telling people how great you are or what you can do for them, and making claims about the results someone can achieve if they go through a procedure with you.

But these days, prospective patients simply don't believe that message. It isn't a unique message. Every service provider in your space is driving home a similar message. And more importantly, none of that proves to a potential patient that you will be able to deliver the results and value that they're looking for.

What does prove you can deliver that value they are looking for is by *demonstrating* it, rather than *claiming* it. Show them that you can help them by *actually* helping them as part of your marketing effort. How do you do this… by leading with value.

For high-valued cosmetic surgery services, at least 80% of your leads won't be ready to buy when they first contact you.

Maybe you meet them at an event and they're interested in your presentation. Or they've come to your website and downloaded your free book, or watched an insightful video of yours. Or maybe they attended a webinar you hosted.

In most cases, that first contact is more about reaching out to gather more information, not a desire to become an immediate buyer.

So, you need to provide more than that, for you to turn that lead into a client.

Instead, you need multiple value-adding interactions. You need to build credibility and trust in specific areas for them to feel ready to buy. And you need to be top of mind when the time is right for them.

This is why value-based marketing is my recommended marketing choice for cosmetic and plastic surgeons who sell high-valued procedures.

A few decades ago, a journalist named Lewis from Jacksonville in the United States, placed the first-ever value-based ad in a small regional newspaper for the financial investment company Merrill Lynch.

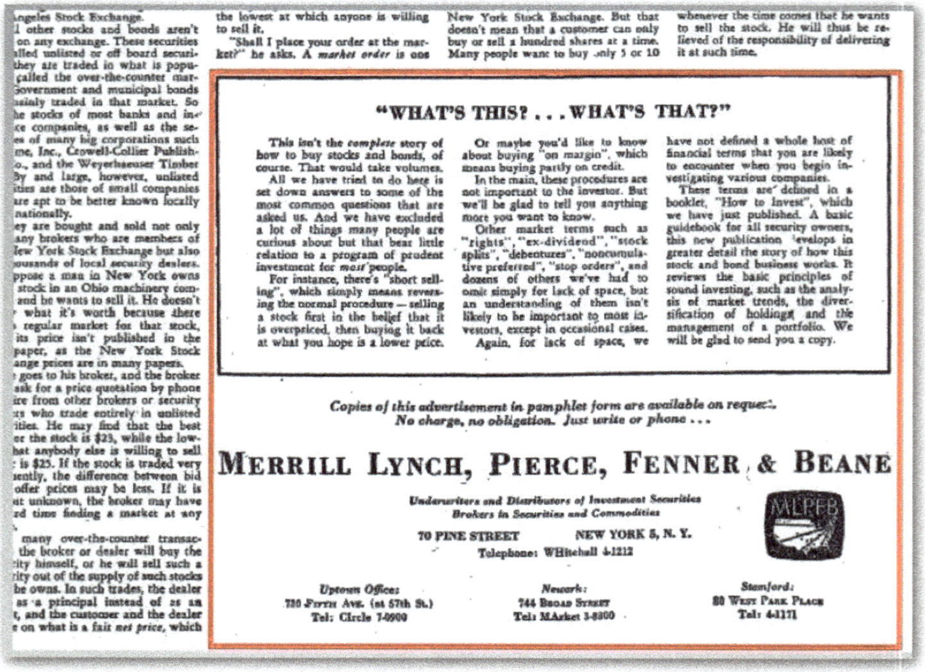

Figure 9: The first successful value-based ad in the world, by Merrill Lynch, featuring a guidebook called "How to Invest", which was offered as a freebie to public investors

The ad campaign was so successful that in its first week of running, the ads pulled in around 5,000 leads. And in the 1950s, they didn't have easy online registration and contact web forms like we have today. This is 5,000 people actually physically cutting out a piece of paper and filling out the form and mailing it back to Merrill Lynch. That is how adding value can gain you more leads.

The greatest ad man in the world—David Ogilvy—later decided to model and perfect this value-based marketing concept. He went on and created 17 ads to sell his own ad agency's services, and those 17 ads helped Ogilvy & Mather sell more than $1.4 billion worth of ad revenue in the 1970s.

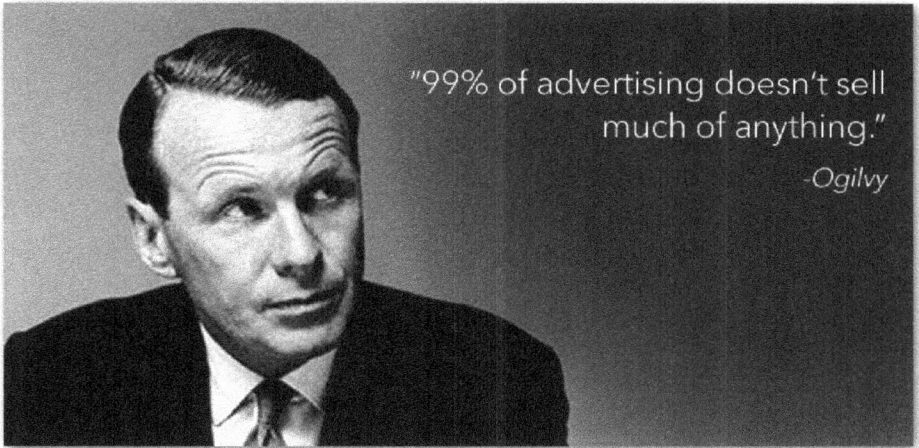

*Figure 10: David Mackenzie Ogilvy CBE was a British advertising tycoon, founder of Ogilvy & Mather, and known as the "Father of Advertising.*

I have been a strong advocate for more value-based marketing initiatives ever since I was first introduced to the concept that one early morning years ago. I think it perfectly suits professionals, especially doctors and surgeons who don't want to come across as sleazy or salesy in their marketing approach.

When you produce content that gives value to your prospects and educates them, you don't need to sell them. Instead, you will be building trust with them, and eventually, they will come to you.

## Type Of Content To Produce

When it comes to value-based marketing initiatives, there are many different types of content that you can produce, including;

- Webinars

- Videos

- Case Studies

- Live Streams

- Podcasts

- Blog Posts

- Reports

- Whitepapers

- Images

People resonate differently to various types of content, but if you are looking to start somewhere, I would suggest starting with moving images first. Any content with visuals and sound will be more engaging than static content: video, webinar, podcast, etc… but if I had to pick just one; my answer is a simple video with captions.

Why captions? Because up to 85% of Facebook video is now watched without sound[1]. We can't expect that everyone who ends up seeing our videos, will be watching it with sound.

I recommend video because I appreciate that you are time-poor, so you need something that you can create quickly, that generates the highest impact. Video can do that, and much more. According to Cisco, video will represent 82% of all internet traffic in 2025.

Over half of all video content is viewed on mobile, and 92% of mobile video viewers share videos with others. People are 10 times more likely to share good video content compared to other photos and blog posts. In short, videos are very powerful.

Plus, you can easily convert or embed video content into other types of content, including;

- Podcasts

- Video blog posts (with transcripts so you can rank on organic search results!)

- Videos used in a newsletter and automated email follow-ups campaign

- Social media (Facebook, Instagram, Tiktok, YouTube, LinkedIn, etc.)

- A Google My Business listing posts

With just one piece of video content, you can use it on many different platforms, and with many different purposes.

---

[1]   https://digiday.com/media/silent-world-facebook-video/

Video is taking over the mobile digital marketing landscape, and video content will be the key driver of a mobile-first marketing strategy this year and onwards.

Are you worried that you won't be able to create great video content? Don't worry. You can create great videos in no time with only a smartphone, and an easy online tool like Capcut for adding captions cheaply, if you need further help, please reach out to marketing@onlinemarketingfordoctors.com.

## How Often Should I Produce Content?

Creating content is one thing, but promoting it is equally important. No use creating great content if it just sits in the folders on your computer. I'll show you how to dominate your online channels with your value-based content in the sections.

You should be committing to producing as much content as you can support through your promotional activities. Your content is the bridge to getting to your target audience. It's the trust-building tool that we use in this online world. That's why I would prefer quality content over quantity.

I suggest creating at least two videos a month. If you can produce more… and support it… please do! You will never suffer from having access to great value-based content.

## What Content Topics Should I Choose?

Content marketing is about creating valuable, relevant content to attract and engage a target audience.

You can always start with your patient's FAQs and the latest news/research about the procedures that your target audience cares most about.

Here are popular types of content you can consider producing:

- Produce educational content about different procedures, recovery processes, and industry trends:

    - Write detailed blog posts explaining common procedures.

    - Create infographics illustrating recovery timelines.

    - Share your expert opinion on emerging trends in cosmetic surgery.

- Create downloadable guides or e-books on popular topics:

    - Example: "What to Expect in a Rhinoplasty Procedure: A Comprehensive Guide"

    - Offer these as free downloads in exchange for email addresses to build your mailing list.

- Start a podcast discussing cosmetic surgery topics and interviewing industry experts:

    - Cover a range of topics from specific procedures to general wellness.

    - Invite colleagues, satisfied patients (with consent), and industry experts as guests.

    - Ensure the podcast is available on major platforms like Spotify and Apple Podcasts.

- Contribute guest articles to reputable health and beauty publications:

  - Target both online and print publications.

  - Focus on providing valuable, educational content rather than overt self-promotion.

  - Use these opportunities to establish yourself as a thought leader in the field.

When you get stuck, you can always check out this amazing tool, www.answerthepuplic.com; that takes your keywords, and gives you the most asked questions and popular search topics online relating to those keywords.

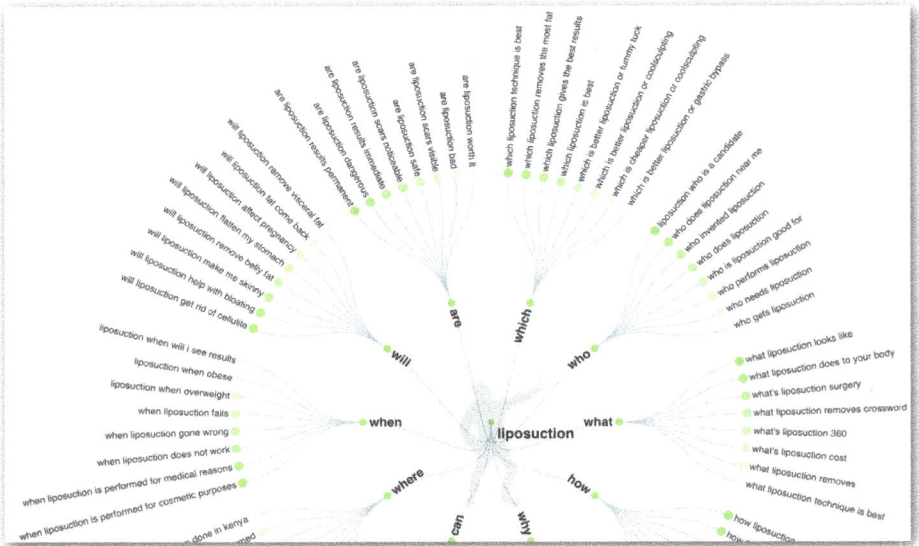

*Figure 11: A comprehensive list of "liposuction" online queries and searches generated by the answerthepublic.com tool*

## Utilise Email Marketing & Build Your Own Database

Email marketing allows for direct communication with potential and existing patients. We often encounter this question from plastic surgeons in the UK: *"If I have a great Instagram page with a lot of followers, do I still need a website?"*

While this is a good question, we need to understand that Instagram is just a rental platform. We are renting a space on Instagram or any other social media channels. Your followers don't belong to you; they belong to Instagram. They can change their algorithm at any time, and you could lose all these followers at any given moment without any prior notice. Your page might get blocked or banned from this platform due to some policy violating issues.

Essentially, you're renting these followers from Instagram or other social channels. Unless you've found ways to convert and transition them into your own database through inbound marketing, you're at risk. This is where a well-designed website with SEO-optimised content that attracts thousands of monthly visitors, along with lead magnets like videos, eBooks, webinars, and events, becomes invaluable.

Email marketing allows you to build and communicate with your own contact database at any time that you want. It gives you control over your audience and your message, something that's not guaranteed on social media platforms.

By developing a strategy that uses social media to funnel followers into your email list, you create a more stable and controllable marketing asset. This approach combines the reach of social media with the reliability and directness of email marketing, providing a more robust long-term strategy for your cosmetic surgery practice.

Here are some key insights from email marketing:

- Build an email list of potential and existing patients:

  - Use opt-in forms on your website and social media.

  - Offer incentives like exclusive content or offers for signing up.

- Send regular newsletters with practice updates, new procedures, and special offers:

  - Maintain a consistent schedule, such as monthly or bi-weekly.

  - Include a mix of educational content, practice news, and promotional offers.

- Use automated email sequences for patient education and follow-ups:

  - Create a welcome series for new subscribers.

  - Develop procedure-specific email sequences to nurture potential patients.

  - Set up post-procedure follow-up emails to support patient recovery and satisfaction.

## Engage with Video Marketing – The Game-Changing Marketing Channel

### 4 Key Benefits of Video Marketing for Cosmetic and Plastic Surgeons

Video marketing offers significant advantages for plastic surgeons specialising in various procedures, from breast augmentation to facelift. Here are four primary benefits:

1. **Humanising Your Practice** Video allows you to showcase your compassion and professionalism before patients step into your surgery. Welcome videos, staff introductions, and virtual tours can help prospective patients feel more at ease, encouraging them to book a consultation.

2. **Building Trust with Patient Testimonials** Authentic patient testimonials are powerful trust-building tools. These videos offer genuine accounts of patient experiences, helping to dispel myths and set realistic expectations for prospective clients.

3. **Demonstrating Expertise** Educational content about procedures, recovery processes, and answering common questions helps establish you as an authority in your field. This approach not only grows your audience but also builds rapport with potential patients.

4. **Enhancing Patient Communication** Videos can be instrumental in converting website visitors to patient consultations and improving patient communication. Use them in email campaigns, on social media, and in your waiting rooms to provide valuable information and encourage bookings.

By leveraging video marketing across various platforms, plastic surgeons can effectively showcase their skills, educate patients, and ultimately increase conversions.

Video content can be particularly effective for cosmetic surgery marketing:

- Create YouTube videos explaining different procedures:

    - Use animations or 3D models to illustrate surgical techniques.

    - Address common questions and concerns about each procedure.

- Use video testimonials from satisfied patients:

    - Ensure you have proper consent and follow GMC guidelines.

    - Showcase a range of procedures and patient demographics.

- Live stream Q&A sessions to engage with potential patients:

    - Host regular live sessions on platforms like YouTube or Instagram.

    - Address common questions and misconceptions about cosmetic procedures.

## STEP 9.  IMPLEMENT LOCAL SEO AND GOOGLE MY BUSINESS

If you've come this far, I know that you've determined the niche that you want to dominate, you've built a professional website and built a social media presence, produced high quality, engaging content and leveraging your mailing lists for generating an ongoing flow of new patient enquiries. I'd like to introduce you to the next essential project for long-term, ongoing investment: search engine optimisation.

## What Is SEO For Cosmetic Surgery Clinics?

SEO can propel your cosmetic surgery clinic to the top of search results on platforms like Google, Yahoo, Bing, and any AI driven search engines. However, the goal extends beyond merely securing a high ranking on search engine results pages; you want your organic visibility to attract high-quality traffic to your site. Quality website traffic ensures that the patients finding your site through search engines are genuinely interested in your cosmetic services or information.

## Why Is SEO Important For Medical Practices?

SEO aligns perfectly with how many patients currently find their surgeons and procedure information online. Without it, you'd miss out on significant opportunities to reach patients actively searching for your services. While referrals still hold value, patients now rely on online resources twice as much as they do on referrals. To position your practice in front of these prospects, a high search engine results page (SERP) ranking is essential.

Top rankings are crucial because the majority of search engine users only pay attention to the first few organic results on Google. In fact, the first five organic listings receive approximately 68% of all clicks (Source of this data is from smartinsights.com).

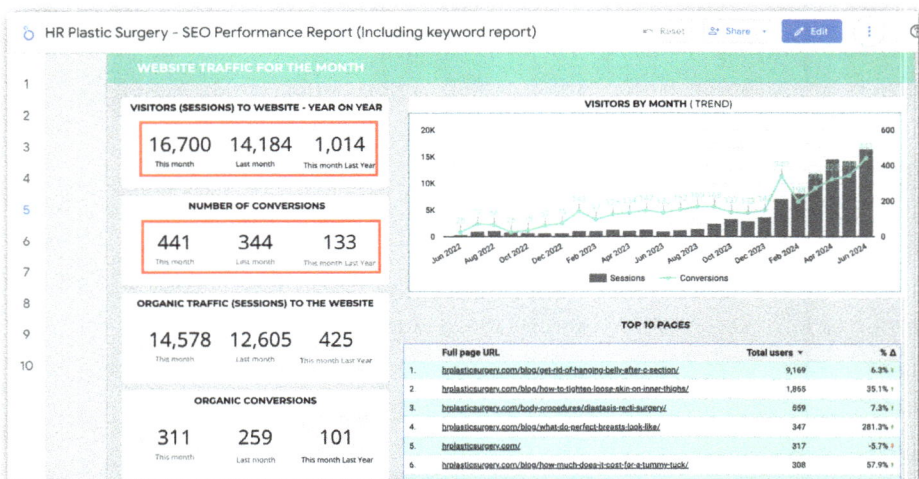

*Figure 12: Growing from 300 to over 16,000 website visitors per month in just two years, with a 400% increase in patient bookings, shows how SEO can be a game-changer for your clinic's marketing.*

## 5 Key Benefits Of SEO For Your Healthcare Practice

### High-Quality Leads:

SEO generates high-quality leads by targeting patients interested in your cosmetic services. For instance, when a user searches for "breast reduction London" on Google, your relevant business pages can appear on the search results if optimised properly. Consequently, the probability of these prospects engaging and converting upon visiting your clinic's website is high.

### Brand Awareness:

Consistently occupying top search result spots boosts brand awareness, even if your website links aren't clicked each time they appear. Consistent exposure helps your practice stay firmly ingrained in the minds of prospective patients.

## Long-Term Affordability or Lower Cost Per New Patient Acquisition:

While paid advertising is an option, it's typically more expensive than SEO in the long run. With SEO, initial costs for meaningful organic traffic are minimal, and well-optimised content continues to attract new patients over time without ongoing pay per visit costs.

## Brand Authority:

SEO contributes to building brand authority, a critical success factor for healthcare businesses. Google recognises high patient engagement levels on your site from relevant search results, establishing your practice as a domain expert in providing meaningful healthcare products or services.

## SEO Helps Your Google Ads Campaign Too:

According to Google, improvements to SEO can help your website rank higher on Google Search by making it more relevant to users. When we utilise one of your existing web pages for the Google Ads campaign or create a new landing page, it's crucial to ensure that relevant keywords are incorporated onto the page. This practice benefits both SEO and Google Ads by improving the quality score of the landing page. Consequently, it enhances the click-through rate of your ads while reducing the cost per click and cost per new patient lead.

If your goal is to drive traffic to your site in the short term, you might choose to focus on paid per click (PPC) ads. If you want to enhance your business's online presence in the long run, SEO is the answer. Alternatively, invest your time and energy in both SEO and PPC for a well-rounded strategy.

## How To Grow Your Practice And Attract More Patients With SEO

You can start implementing effective SEO strategies can help your practice rank higher:

- Publish meaningful content that answers prospective patients' search engine queries.

- Publish keyword-optimised content to ensure that your website and services rank for target patients' search intent.

- Optimise your content and your site for local search because most patients seek medical help at facilities near where they live, this includes your Google My Business listings too.

- Build high-quality backlinks to boost your SERP rankings and increase organic traffic to your website.

An effective SEO strategy for medical practices entails publishing relevant, keyword-optimised content on your standard webpages, blogs and landing pages. Ask yourself, *"What phrases would a patient search for on Google when looking for services like mine?"* By getting your strategy right, you can increase your practice's online visibility and website engagement, helping you bring in more new patients.

By developing and implementing a sound SEO strategy, you can boost your practice's online visibility, engage website visitors, and attract more new patients.

With Online Marketing For Doctors' digital marketing strategy for medical practices – we develop a full-funnel approach which relies on more consistent ongoing engagement, even for SEO.

This SEO content funnel will help guide your potential clients' journey from brand awareness to consideration, conversion, and even loyalty and advocacy after they become a client or patient at your clinic. It's a holistic SEO content strategy that goes beyond the typical digital marketing approach.

The OMD
Full Funnel
STRATEGY

AWARENESS
CONSIDERATION
CONVERSION
LOYALTY
ADVOCACY

*Figure 13: OMD Full Funnel Digital Marketing Strategy*

## Leveraging Google My Business for Your Cosmetic Clinic

Google My Business (GMB) is an essential tool for cosmetic and plastic surgeons looking to enhance their local online presence. This free platform offers numerous benefits:

1. **Improved Local Visibility:** GMB listings often appear in the "Local Pack" at the top of search results, increasing your chances of being seen by potential patients in your area.

2. **Enhanced Credibility:** A complete GMB profile with reviews and accurate information builds trust with potential patients.

3. **Direct Patient Engagement**: GMB allows you to respond to reviews and messages directly, fostering better patient According to Google, improvements to SEO relationships.

4. **Valuable Insights:** Google provides data on how patients find and interact with your listing, helping you refine your marketing strategy.

5. **Mobile Optimisation:** GMB listings are prominently displayed in mobile search results, crucial as more patients use smartphones to find healthcare providers.

6. **Integration with Google Maps:** Your practice becomes easily findable on Google Maps, helping patients locate you effortlessly.

To maximise these benefits, optimising for local search can significantly boost your visibility:

- Optimise your Google My Business listing:

  - Ensure all information is accurate and up-to-date.

  - Regularly post updates, offers, and events.

- Encourage satisfied patients to leave Google reviews:

  - Implement a system to request reviews post-procedure.

  - Respond professionally to all reviews, both positive and negative.

- Ensure consistent NAP (Name, Address, Phone) information:

  - Check all online directories and update as necessary.

  - Use schema markup on your website to help search engines understand your business information.

By effectively leveraging GMB and following these optimisation strategies, cosmetic surgeons can significantly enhance their local online presence, attract more potential patients, and build stronger relationships with their existing patient base.

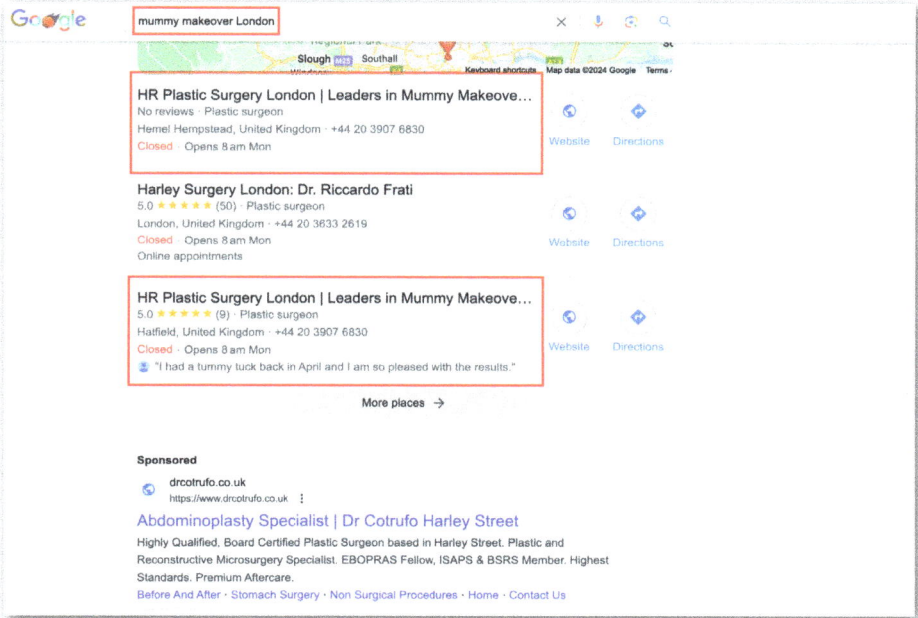

*Figure 14: Example of HR Plastic Surgery Top Ranking on Google Maps For "Mummy Makeover London"*

## BONUS STRATEGY: PAID ADVERTISING – GOOGLE, META & MORE

Now, let's talk about Google Ads first as it is quite similar to Bing Ads. What exactly are they? Well, think of Google Ads as your practice's digital billboard on the world's busiest highway - the internet. It's an online advertising platform that lets you create targeted ads appearing on Google search results, websites, YouTube, Gmail and more.

When potential patients search for keywords related to your services, your ads can pop up right at the top of the search results. But advances in Google's AI technology also means you can reach prospects in many more places too.

But why should you, as a plastic surgeon, care about paid per click advertising (PPC)? Let me break it down for you:

First off, it's all about reaching your target audience. With Google Ads, you can laser-focus your ads on people searching for specific medical conditions or treatments. It's like having a megaphone that only the right people can hear. Google and Meta (Facebook and Instagram platforms) are the two biggest players in the online advertising space, so getting this right can unlock huge growth opportunities.

**Secondly, it's a brand awareness booster.** The more people see your practice name in their search results, the more familiar and trustworthy you become in their eyes.

Third, it's a traffic driver. When people click on your ads, they land on your website, where they can learn more about your expertise and hopefully book an appointment. This is especially important if you're just starting out with SEO, as it can take at least 12 months to begin to really bear fruit. When you need a short-term boost to your website visitors, Google Ads is a great way to achieve that.

**And let's not forget about improving conversions.** By tracking your ad results, you can fine-tune your approach and turn more clicks into actual patients walking through your door.

Strategic paid advertising can complement your organic marketing efforts:

- Utilise Google Ads for search and display advertising:

  - Target specific keywords related to cosmetic procedures.

  - Use ad extensions to include additional information like phone numbers or links to specific pages.

- Use Meta retargeting ads:

  - Set up Meta ads campaigns to reach people who have visited your website, who are on your email list or your existing social media followers and their lookalike audience.

  - Create specific ads for different procedures or pages they've viewed.

## BONUS STRATEGY: INFLUENCER PARTNERSHIPS FOR MODERN VISIBILITY

Influencer marketing in plastic surgery offers numerous benefits for practitioners looking to expand their reach and credibility. By partnering with respected influencers in beauty, wellness, or lifestyle niches, surgeons can tap into large, engaged audiences that are often already interested in cosmetic procedures.

These collaborations provide a platform for visual showcases of results and personal testimonials, which can be more relatable and convincing than traditional advertising. Influencers can help educate potential patients about procedures, set trends in cosmetic surgery, and even work to normalise discussions around these topics, potentially overcoming stigma.

The visual nature of social media platforms used by influencers aligns well with the before-and-after narrative crucial in plastic surgery marketing. Additionally, influencer partnerships can be a cost-effective marketing strategy, especially for reaching younger demographics, and often generate higher engagement rates than brand-created content. This increased visibility and engagement can lead to more enquiries and potentially new patients for plastic surgery practices.

Collaborating with influencers can expand your reach, but must be approached carefully:

- Collaborate with micro-influencers in the beauty and wellness space:

  - Focus on influencers with engaged followings rather than just large numbers.

  - Ensure the influencer's values align with your practice's ethos.

  - Check the influencer's feed and previous posts and ask yourself if they align with your brand's aesthetic and values. Make sure their content is informative and well produced.

  - Authenticity: Look for influencers who have a genuine interest in cosmetic procedures and have potentially successfully worked with other medical professionals. They will be more familiar with the unique requirements and restrictions in this field.

- Offer influencers treatments in exchange for honest reviews and content:

  - Be clear about expectations and deliverables.

  - Encourage authentic, balanced reviews rather than overly promotional content.

- Ensure all partnerships comply with advertising standards and medical ethics guidelines:

  - Familiarise yourself with ASA (Advertising Standards Authority) guidelines.

  - Ensure all sponsored content is clearly labelled as such.

- Consider these various collaboration types to keep your influencer marketing fresh and engaging:

  - Treatment Reviews: Influencers document their experience with a specific procedure.

  - Educational Content Series: Partner with influencers to create informative content about different procedures, precare and aftercare.

  - Q&A Sessions: During these sessions, the host influencer and the practice's audience interact in real time and ask questions about procedures or general cosmetic surgery topics.

  - Long-term Ambassadorships: For a sustained plan and impact, consider establishing longer-term relationships with select influencers who can become advocates for your practice.

## CONCLUSION: BUILDING YOUR DREAM PRACTICE WITH THE RIGHT PARTNER

Throughout this guide, we've explored nine critical steps to establishing and growing a thriving private cosmetic surgery practice in the UK. From defining your target market and specialty procedures to leveraging digital marketing strategies and building your online reputation, each element plays a vital role in your practice's success.

However, if there's one overarching lesson that emerges from the experiences shared by successful surgeons like Mr. Alfie, Dr. Khademi, and Mr. Mouzakis, it's this: the team you choose to support your journey can make or break your practice.

As Mr. Alfie wisely noted, *"I should have focused solely on my surgical practice instead of splitting my attention with business management. Collaborating with a professional marketing firm earlier on would have been a smarter move than trying to manage marketing and IT on my own."*

This sentiment echoes throughout the experiences of many surgeons who have walked this path before you. Your exceptional surgical skills are the foundation of your practice, but trying to handle everything yourself—from website development to SEO strategy to patient journey mapping—often leads to suboptimal results and unnecessary stress.

The most successful plastic surgeons recognise that building a practice requires a constellation of specialised skills that no single individual can master. Just as you've spent years perfecting your surgical techniques, marketing specialists, web developers, and practice management experts have invested time in mastering their respective crafts.

When selecting partners for your journey, consider these critical factors:

1. **Specialisation:** Choose partners who understand the unique challenges and opportunities within the cosmetic surgery industry. Generic marketing agencies or web developers often lack the specialised knowledge needed to navigate the complexities of medical marketing regulations and patient psychology.

2. **Proven Results:** Look for partners with a track record of success specifically within your field.

3. **Long-Term Vision:** Seek partners who can grow with you, from your initial steps into private practice through to scaling a thriving clinic. The best partnerships evolve alongside your practice's development.

4. **Value-Driven Approach:** As Dr. Naveen Somia mentioned about our approach at Online Marketing For Doctors, *"Every time she had the option to go with the more expensive version, she always recommended the cheaper version with the view of adding value to me as the client."* Choose partners who prioritise your success over maximising their profits.

Remember, establishing a private practice is not a sprint but a marathon. The right partners won't simply offer quick fixes; they'll provide strategic guidance, honest feedback, and sustainable systems that build toward long-term success.

As Warren Buffett wisely said, *"Someone's sitting in the shade today because someone planted a tree a long time ago."*

*Figure 15: During her MBA studies in the United States, Huyen Truong had the opportunity to meet Warren Buffett.*

Your decisions today about which partners to trust with specific aspects of your practice development will shape your success for years to come.

This journey requires persistence—the same persistence that has brought you through medical school, surgical training, and to this point in your career. By focusing your energy on surgical excellence while delegating specialised tasks to proven experts, you position yourself for the greatest possible success.

Now, armed with these nine essential steps and the wisdom to choose the right partners, you're ready to establish and grow the thriving private practice you've always envisioned. The path ahead will have challenges, but with the right team supporting your journey, you'll navigate them successfully.

The best time to start is now.

# SPECIAL BONUS - WHAT OTHER UK SURGEONS THINK?

*Remark from Mr Hazem Alfie*
*- MBBCh, MSc, FRCS Plastic Surgery, Delta Clinics UK*
*www.deltaclinics.co.uk*

*Hi Huyen,*

*Reflecting on my journey, I realise I would have taken a different approach to setting up my practice. Utilising existing facilities, such as hospitals or locations on Harley Street, would have been a more cost-effective strategy than setting up my own theatre.*

*My time spent on non clinical activities have tripled and it has become not cost effective. It would have been more beneficial to have spent most of my time in clinical matters.*

*The financial demands of operating a private theatre are significant; it needs to be in use 5-7 days a week to break even. When it's only used 1-2 days a week, the losses can accumulate rapidly. Once you commit to a private clinic with a theatre, you're often stuck in contracts and expenses that are hard to escape. This is a prevalent issue in the UK healthcare system, where many hospitals find themselves operating at a loss due to long-term contracts that make closure impractical.*

*I should have focused solely on my surgical practice instead of splitting my attention with business management.* ***Collaborating with a professional marketing firm like Online Marketing for Doctors earlier on would have been a smarter move than trying to manage marketing and IT on my own or hiring a one-man-band IT person or web developer.***

*A key takeaway for me was the **importance of pricing strategy; I should have established premium rates from the beginning.***

*My main advice for new practitioners is simple: prioritise surgical excellence, establish high prices, collaborate with professional marketers from the start, and steer clear of the challenges that come with running a full-service clinic if you can.*

*Regards,*
*Hazem Alfie*
*MBBCh, MSc, FRCS Plastic Surgery*
*Delta Clinics UK*

### Introduction:

*Mr. Alfie is an experienced cosmetic surgeon who has worked in hospitals across the UK, Qatar, and Egypt, holding roles such as Consultant Plastic and Breast Reconstruction Surgeon at Bedfordshire Hospitals NHS trust, Plastic and Hand Surgery Consultant at University Hospitals Coventry & Warwickshire and Breast Reconstruction Fellow at Whiston Hospital, Liverpool. He continually updates his skills by attending educational courses, conferences, and presenting at national and international meetings. He has also contributed to specialist publications.*

*Committed to patient care, all surgeons, including Mr. Alfie, are registered with the General Medical Council (GMC), undergo annual appraisals, and hold practising privileges under strict clinical governance. Despite their extensive experience, they prioritise making each patient's experience as positive as their treatment outcome.*

*Remark from Mr Michael P. Mouzakis*
*- Dr Mooz Clinic*
*www.drmooz.com*

*Hi Huyen,*

*This is a very interesting thing and I would be delighted to assist you with.*

**I think the main thing is to learn and master one or maximum two procedures in the field of cosmetic surgery.**

*It is super important to show to your future patients that someone has dealt with numerous cases of the same procedure and as a surgeon you have a solid experience in it.*

**At the same time getting accredited, staying up to date and doing more and more procedures** *will lead to standardising the pathway and improve the patient's experience to the maximum level.*

*Offering all sorts of treatments is like being in a touristic restaurant in a populated city like the centre of Rome.*

*But if you want to have the best food you need to look for a restaurant with a very short menu and a couple Michelin stars.*

*Happy to tell you more!*
*Warm regards,*
*Mr Michael P. Mouzakis*

*Consultant in Plastic Reconstructive and Aesthetic Surgery , Master of Science in Aesthetic Medicine at Queen Mary University of London*

**Introduction:**

*Mr Michael Mouzakis is an award-winning Plastic Surgeon with more than 15 years' experience and recognised for his skill, experience and meticulous approach.*

*He is highly rated by his patients for the results he delivers in hair restoration, body contouring, facial rejuvenation and breast enhancement.*

*He is a fully accredited Plastic Surgeon, board certified by the GMC and the Hellenic Medical Association, who practices as a consultant in the private sector. He holds a consultant post at The Private Clinic of Harley Street and at London Plastic Surgery in Athens.*

*Learn more about him and his clinic on www.drmooz.com*

## *Remark from Dr Arash Khademi*
### *- Dr Kay Clinic*
### *www.drkayclinic.com*

*Dear Huyen,*

*Thank you for reaching out and for your interest in my journey. Writing a book to help UK surgeons transition into the private sector is a fantastic initiative, and I'm happy to share my thoughts. Reflecting on my experience, there are two significant areas that I wish I had prioritised or executed differently when building my private practice:*

### 1. Investing Early in a Strong Online Presence

*One of the most valuable lessons I've learned is the importance of a professional, user-friendly website and a robust digital marketing strategy from the outset. When I started, I underestimated how much influence an effective online presence would have in shaping patient perceptions and driving inquiries. In hindsight, here are the key elements I would have focused on sooner:*

*SEO Optimisation: Ensuring my website was optimised for search engines from the start to attract local traffic. Patients often begin their search online, and ranking highly for relevant terms like "cosmetic surgery in London" or "aesthetic treatments near me" would have accelerated patient acquisition.*

*Educational Content: Creating valuable, patient-focused content such as blogs, FAQs, and videos explaining procedures. This not only builds trust but also positions you as a thought leader in the field.*

*Social Media Strategy: Engaging consistently on platforms like Instagram, LinkedIn, and YouTube to showcase results, educate potential patients, and humanise the practice.*

*If I had embraced this earlier, I believe the growth of my clinic would have been more rapid and efficient.*

### 2. Building Strategic Partnerships and Expanding Offerings

*Early on, I focused solely on delivering exceptional treatments, which is, of course, critical. However, I now realise the value of building partnerships and offering complementary services that enhance the patient experience. Two things I wish I had done sooner:*

*Collaborations: Partnering with wellness professionals, gyms, and yoga studios earlier could have expanded my reach to a broader patient base and aligned my practice with holistic well-being. These collaborations bring mutual benefits and drive patient referrals.*

*Diversifying Services: Introducing complementary services like IV nutrient therapy, skin health programs, or even minimally-invasive body contouring sooner would have catered to a wider range of patient needs and boosted retention rates. Patients often look for clinics that offer a comprehensive range of treatments under one roof.*

### Bonus Thought: Understanding the Patient Journey

*Lastly, I wish I had mapped the entire patient journey from inquiry to aftercare much earlier. Streamlining processes like appointment scheduling, consultations, and follow-ups—while ensuring top-notch customer service—plays a pivotal role in patient satisfaction and retention. Investing in a high-quality CRM system from the beginning would have made this much easier.*

*I hope this insight proves useful for your book. Building a private practice is undoubtedly a journey of continuous learning, and I look forward to seeing your book help others navigate this transition successfully. Please let me know if I can assist further or contribute more perspectives.*

*Kind regards,*
*Dr Arash Khademi*
*Dr Kay Clinic*

### Introduction:

*Dr Arash Khademi (Dr K.) is a London cosmetic surgeon & senior international trainer in aesthetic medicine and surgery with 27 years of clinical, academic, management, and leadership experience. He is the Key Opinion Leader (KOL) of Euromi, Promoitalia, T-Lab, and Hawksley; All leading international companies in aesthetic medicine and surgery.*

*Learn more about him and his clinic on www.drkayclinic.com*

# ABOUT AUTHOR
# HUYEN TRUONG, MBA

*Search Marketing Strategist/Founder*
*Online Marketing For Doctors*

Hi, I'm Huyen Truong

I'm Australian. I have lived and worked on three different continents, but I was born and raised in Vietnam in a poor working-class family during the de-centralising economic period of the 1990s. It was very tough back then.

I have walked a path that few other entrepreneurs have.

My parents worked very hard juggling various business ventures just to put food on the table.

I learnt a valuable thing from my parents' success.

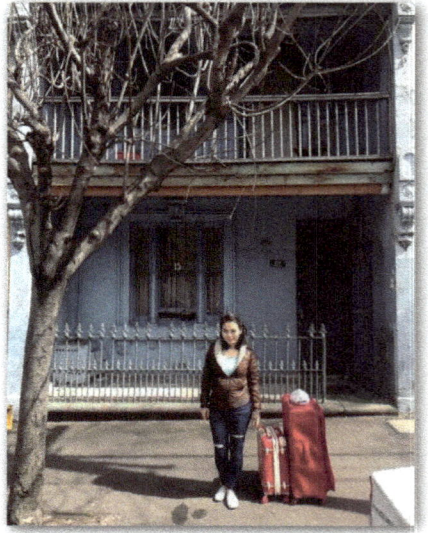

One word. Persistence.

Nothing in this world can take the place of good old persistence.

Talent won't.
Genius won't.
Education won't.

Persistence and determination are all-powerful.

They are the principles that enabled my parents to rise up in their lives when most people their age were giving up or thinking about retirement.

Growing up, I saw them trying many different types of businesses and opportunities until they finally experienced a breakthrough with one of their businesses when they were in their late 40s.

My parents had finally turned a business into a multi-million dollar business. But it took a long time to get there.

Persistence.

It was in this humble beginning that inspired me to dream of a better future for myself, and I picked up my business sense from them.

I started selling candy for money when I was 5. I was trying to sell things around me as much as possible to make any extra cash I could to buy treats that my parents were unable to afford at the time. The entrepreneurial spirit inside of me was unleashed very early on, and I haven't looked back.

I had even started selling online advertising in the early 2000s when online marketing was still in its infancy, as I knew back then it would be the future of marketing.

Through many years of working hard and saving money, my parents were able to send me to the United States for graduate education. I graduated from the University of Missouri-Columbia with an MBA during one of the worst financial crises, 2008–2010.

But during that financial crisis, instead of choosing to stay in America and trying to survive there, I decided to make a bold move by packing my bags and moving to Australia. It's something none of my classmates even considered.

I moved to Australia in 2011 as a poor student without any connections, no job, money, or family and friends—just two suitcases and more than $US 100,000 in student debt.

I started out sharing a room with another student, living in a tiny old house with 8 other students, with no heater and just one bathroom to share. Every night, I could feel the cold, high-pitched whistling winds blowing through the rattling bedroom window, keeping me awake at night. Life didn't look so promising back then.

But I had this dream on the first day I stepped foot in Australia of creating a leading digital marketing agency, and that dream has kept me going until today.

Back then, I had no idea how to make it happen, but I just knew deep down that I was going to achieve it someday.

I started small, slowly building a reputation by working on multiple jobs helping small businesses with their search marketing. Result Driven SEO was the first agency I founded, and while it didn't happen overnight, it started growing bigger and bigger.

But it grew to a point when I realised that the competition in this broad industry was getting really fierce. The competition was everywhere, and everyone was chasing any potential client making any wild promise they could just to land them.

It was in those moments that I began to understand the value of specialising in one niche and how it could set my agency apart from my competitors. That's why I founded Online Marketing for Doctors (OMD) and Queen of Cosmetic Marketing, to claim my celebrity authority on a niche industry that I knew very well.

This company has since grown incredibly well over time, and I couldn't be prouder of the work that my wonderful OMD team has done to support cosmetic and plastic surgeons around the world, to achieve their own dreams for their practices. It has been incredibly satisfying work.

But the tale doesn't end here. It is constantly being rewritten every day with new exciting challenges and opportunities in this dynamically changing and ever-growing industry. And I plan on continuing to push forward, striving to be the best that I can be, in the same fighting spirit that my wonderful parents instilled in me those many years ago.

Persistence.

# ABOUT ONLINE MARKETING FOR DOCTORS

## LEADING SEARCH MARKETING & LEAD GENERATION FIRM FOR MEDICAL CLINICS.

Online Marketing For Doctors is a specialised digital marketing agency focused exclusively on generating new patients for medical clinics.

From reconstructive-turned-cosmetic surgeons to young, thriving plastic surgeons to world-renowned plastic surgeons or presidents of the, British Association of Aesthetic Plastic Surgeons, Australasian and American Society of Aesthetic Plastic Surgeons, we have helped them all to succeed in online lead generation and build a strong and resilient brand in this hyper-competitive aesthetic industry.

We have built a dream team designed for building incredible aesthetic clinics' digital marketing campaigns. You get to work with specialists, not generalists.

The quality and results of your campaign are second to none, as your success is our ultimate goal and the reason for our existence.

**Our Core Values:**

- ☑ **Responsive**
- ☑ **Thorough**
- ☑ **Results Driven**
- ☑ **Proactive**
- ☑ **Accountable**

We are known by our clients for our five core qualities:

We work hard to ensure that these qualities are carried throughout our working process with all of our clients.

I was lucky to meet Warren Buffet—billionaire and legendary investor—when I was doing my MBA in the USA, and he told us this;

*"Someone's sitting in the shade today because someone planted a tree a long time ago."* - **Warren Buffet**

Ever since then, I've always wanted to plant a tree, a tree of a proven marketing system and framework for cosmetic and plastic surgeons around the world that they can use, so that they can enjoy the benefits that come with successfully growing and scaling their practice.

If you are interested in speaking with me and my team, please book a call with us.

Book a Strategy Call With Online Marketing For Doctors Team

# WHAT OTHER SURGEONS SAY ABOUT US

## BREAST AND BODY CLINIC UK

*"Since working with Online Marketing for Doctors my website has gone from 300 visitors a day to over 5,000 visitors a day. I wasn't on the first page for any of my main keywords and now I'm on the first page for all of them.* **The website conversion number has gone up by 618% compared to the same time last year.**

**Mr Aftab Siddiqui**
*Plastic Surgeon/Owner of Breast and Body Clinic*
*www.breastandbodyclinic.co.uk*

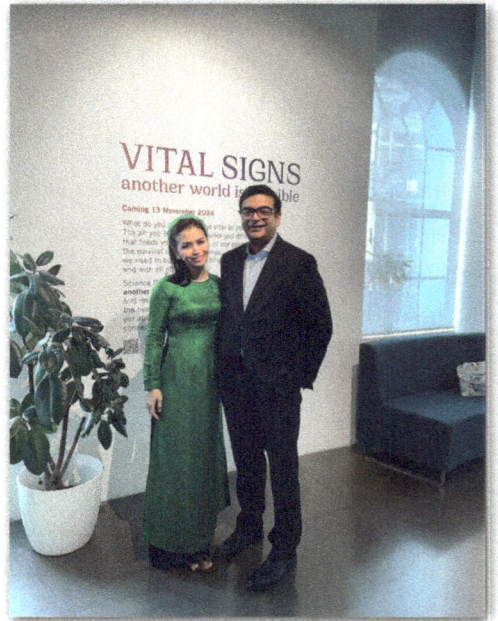

*Watch The Testimonial Video*

## HR PLASTIC SURGERY

*Over the past 2 years, we are thrilled with the outcomes. OMD successfully secured our ranking for highly competitive keywords, **driving over 16,000 monthly visitors to our website. The conversion numbers witnessed an impressive surge of 400% across all traffic channels.** In comparison to the initial state of my website, OMD not only met but exceeded my expectations.*

**Mr Hyder Ridha**
*Plastic Surgeon/Owner of HR Plastic Surgery*
www.hrplasticsurgery.com

Watch The Testimonial Video

## DELTA CLINICS UK

*"I'm Hazem Alfie, I'm a consultant plastic surgeon. I'm based in Harley Street and in Finchley, London, in the United Kingdom. I specialise in plastic and cosmetic surgery procedures. I've been a consultant myself for 19 years and we have got a good team of staff members who work with us.*

*We have been working exclusively with Online Marketing for Doctors for the last eight months, we have seen amazing results with them. They are hands on, they are very approachable and they are very able to do what they promise. They have been delivering what we have agreed on before the start.* **I have seen an increase of almost 730% in the total number of leads or inquiries that come to the clinic, and this also reflects on the total number of patients that I see for consultations.**

*And also reflects on the total number of patients I've been operating on that also have increased over the last eight months.*

*Currently they are managing our website, they have designed a totally new website, they have also been doing our SEO and I've seen great results with the SEO and they have recently taken our social media management and the reflects the trust I have in them.*

*The rest of Delta Clinic's team like dealing with OMD team members that are designated for Delta Clinics. They have not had any problems with them and I enjoy working with them and I am looking for a long-term partnership.*

*I would definitely recommend them. Despite saying that everyone in the team has been amazing and brilliant there are two people that I would like definitely to extend my thanks to. These are Martina and Louise. Martina is being very approachable. Whenever I sent her a message, she always responded. She works really hard and I feel that she cares about my business, not only her business. Louise also has been spending a lot of time in creating my content and then revising the SEO continuously, producing great reports. So especially to these two, thank you very much."*

**Mr. Hazem Alfie**

*MBBCh, MSc, FRCS Plastic Surgery*
*Consultant Plastic Surgeon*
*Delta Clinics London, UK*
*www.deltaclinics.co.uk*

*Watch The Testimonial Video*

## DR NAVEEN SOMIA

*"What I saw was the ranking slowly starting to climb and we were very happy with the way the rankings were going, especially for some of the keywords that I wanted to be on the first page of Google.*

*That translated into a lot of visitors coming to my website. Over the **last 12 months** we have increased **the web traffic by over 100% and also increased the conversions by 100%.***

*And so far, I'm happy with the progress that we have made. And the one nice thing about Huyen is that every time she had the option to go with the more expensive version, she always recommended the cheaper version with the view of adding value to me as the client, which is very reassuring and a lot different from what my experiences have been in the past."*

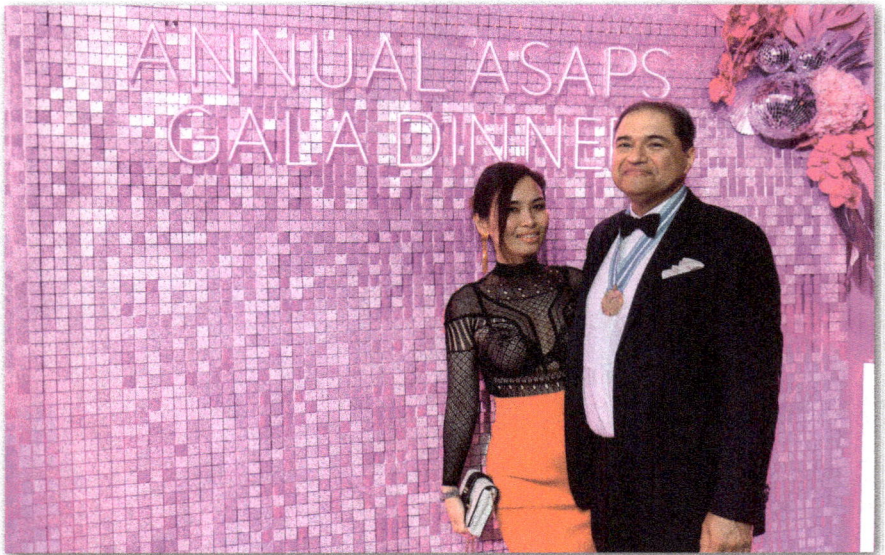

**Dr Naveen Somia**
*MBBS, PhD, FRACS*
*Cosmetic & Plastic/Reconstructive Surgeon/ ASAPS President*

*Watch The Testimonial Video*

## BRITISH FACE CLINIC

*"I'm Mr. Supriya on behalf of British face clinic. We have been working with OMD for the last year and we have seen a significant change in our practice success. OMD completely renovated our website and gave it a much fresher look. They have also helped us with our SEO and with our paid Google campaign and we have seen significant increase in our organic traffic which has grown by around 150%.*

*And similarly, we have seen a significant **increase in our organic keywords, which has grown by 1,000%. We have seen an increase in our practice with a ROI of around 5.08.***

*So hopefully we will continue to work together and will see further enhancements in our performance."*

**Mr Mrinal Supriya**
*Facial Cosmetic Surgeon,*
*FRCS (OTOL-HNS), MRCS Ed, DO-HNS, MS in ENT, MBBS*
*www.britishfaceclinic.com*

Watch The Testimonial Video

## CROWN CLINIC

*We have been using the Online Marketing for Doctors team **since 2019** and we are very happy with the results. They put together a comprehensive strategy and plan to improve our digital marketing presence (SEO, PPC ads, Social Media, Website Content and Landing Pages), and so far we can see obviously improved results from the work that they have done. **Enquiries have gone crazy and the number of enquiries has increased three-fold ever since they started within the first year.** The team and Huyen have been very responsive to support us along the way with our IT problems, they are very thorough and results-driven with their work. We would highly recommend them.*

**James Nadin**
*CEO of ICCM & Crown Clinic*

*Watch The Testimonial Video*

www.ingramcontent.com/pod-product-compliance
Lightning Source LLC
Chambersburg PA
CBHW040929210326
41597CB00030B/5232